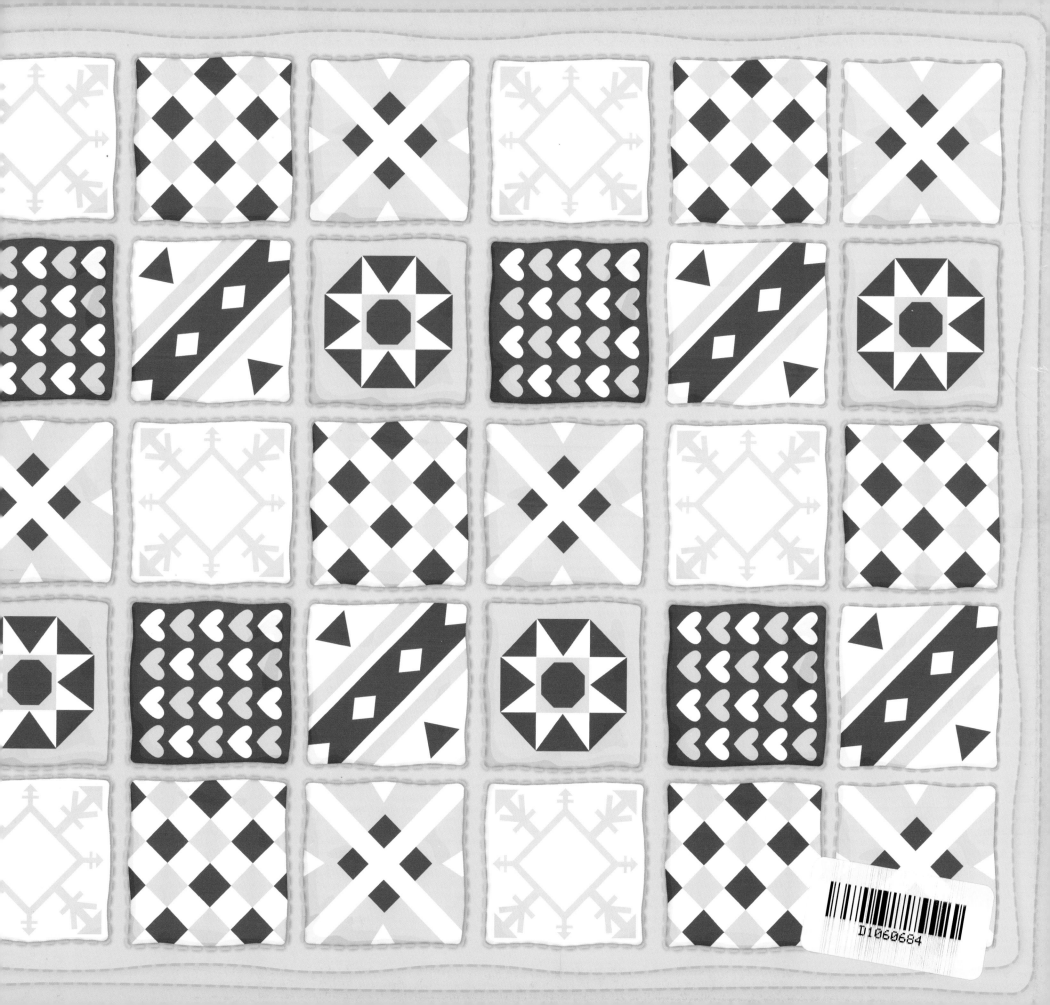

This Book Belongs to....

THE GREAT MRS. CLAUS

WRITTEN BY CHRIS A. SHOEMAKER   ILLUSTRATED BY CESAR DE CASTRO

Written by Chris A. Shoemaker
Copyright © 2008 Chris A. Shoemaker
Illustration & Map by Cesar De Castro
Illustrations copyright © Claus Family Christmas, LLC
Book & Cover Design/Graphics and Painting by Art Baez
North Pole Map Design & Painting by Marvin Ying-Lin Chow & Crystal Thomas
Additional Painting by Lucas Steadman
Edited by Ruth Strother
Contributing Editor: Suzanne Shoemaker
Photo of Chris Shoemaker by Carol Gehring
Photo of Cesar De Castro by Chris Shoemaker
The Claus Diaries & Claus Seal Graphic by William Kent
Illustrations, logos & graphics © 2008 The Claus Family Christmas, LLC

Published by

THE Claus Family
CHRISTMAS, LLC

For information address
The Claus Family Christmas, LLC
24307 Magic Mountain Parkway #504
Santa Clarita, California 91355

Reinforced binding. Printed and bound in China
First Edition

Library of Congress Control Number: 2007905763

ISBN 978-0-9798186-6-0

Visit: TheClausDiaries.com

The Claus Diaries is an imprint of
The Claus Family Christmas, LLC

ACKNOWLEDGMENT

To Suzanne–my great Mrs. Claus & spectacular friend

To Mother–a better Muse no son could have. Your steadfast spirit shines the way

To Tyler–through the years, your ever-so-wise Sparky inspired us all

My deepest heartfelt thanks to these true Believers:

Faye & Dave Crunkilton, Tom Carnahan, Lee Ann Crider,
Harry & Elaine Hillier, Herbert & Aileen Spearman,
Janis Salin & Jim Woloshyn, Michael Dumbaugh, Christopher Welch,
Cesar & Aurea De Castro, Art & Marie Baez, Crystal Thomas,
Ruth & Stephanie Strother, William Kent, Jon Rosenberg, Patte Dee McKee,
Bill J. Gottlieb, Hannah & Page Langley, K C Kappen, Timothy Linh Bui,
Sindee Pickens, Marjorie Crowley, Gwendolyn Ballantyne,
Marvin Ying-Lin Chow, Luc Steadman, and Leo Lotz

–C.A.S.

The List of the North Pole Daytime Landmarks

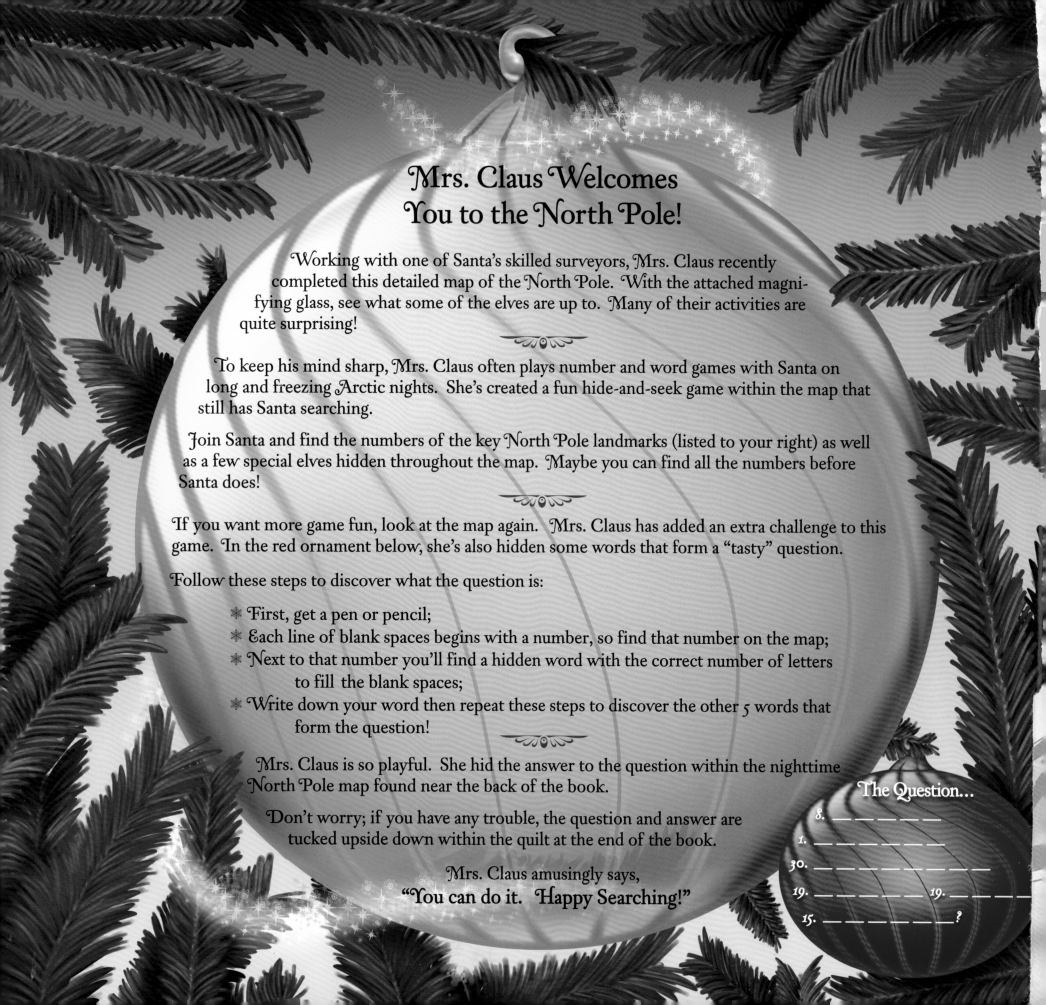

Mrs. Claus Welcomes
You to the North Pole!

Working with one of Santa's skilled surveyors, Mrs. Claus recently completed this detailed map of the North Pole. With the attached magnifying glass, see what some of the elves are up to. Many of their activities are quite surprising!

To keep his mind sharp, Mrs. Claus often plays number and word games with Santa on long and freezing Arctic nights. She's created a fun hide-and-seek game within the map that still has Santa searching.

Join Santa and find the numbers of the key North Pole landmarks (listed to your right) as well as a few special elves hidden throughout the map. Maybe you can find all the numbers before Santa does!

If you want more game fun, look at the map again. Mrs. Claus has added an extra challenge to this game. In the red ornament below, she's also hidden some words that form a "tasty" question.

Follow these steps to discover what the question is:

❋ First, get a pen or pencil;
❋ Each line of blank spaces begins with a number, so find that number on the map;
❋ Next to that number you'll find a hidden word with the correct number of letters to fill the blank spaces;
❋ Write down your word then repeat these steps to discover the other 5 words that form the question!

Mrs. Claus is so playful. She hid the answer to the question within the nighttime North Pole map found near the back of the book.

Don't worry; if you have any trouble, the question and answer are tucked upside down within the quilt at the end of the book.

Mrs. Claus amusingly says,
"You can do it. Happy Searching!"

The Question...

8. _ _ _ _ _

1. _ _ _ _ _ _

30. _ _ _ _ _ _ _

19. _ _ _ _ _ _   19. _ _ _ _

15. _ _ _ _ _ _ _ ?

Welcome Youth

To move this page is quite a tussle,
for three strong elves with lots of muscle.

Of All Ages

POSTING BOX

With ease
two reindeer
turn this
paper
to reveal the
place where
young elves
caper.

"On your mark, get set. . ." KA-BOOM! The starter's canon thundered through the crisp morning air. Sleds hit the snow. The race was on. Dozens of young elves flew down the north slopes of Glitterlit Mountain with snow tails arched high behind their zigzagging sleds. Bystanders cheered on their favorite sled riders till their voices were hoarse. The racers furiously pumped their legs and lunged with all their might to cross the finish line first. Rassle's sled shot through the air like a rocket. Winning this race seemed a matter of life or death.

In a young elf's life, nothing beats winning Santa's Glitterlit Downhill Sled Race. Besides earning bragging rights as the "fastest and most respected elf on a sled," the top prize includes a one-year break from the tedious chore of wood chopping. Elves avoided wood chopping like a bad arctic cold.

As Sparky stared out of his frosted workshop window, he daydreamed about Rassle winning the race. An icicle suddenly fell from the roof and shattered like a fine crystal glass into hundreds of pieces. Startled, Sparky blinked and his exhilarating daydream quickly vanished. "You can win it Rassle!" he cheered out loud to himself. He chuckled at his own boyish excitement. Time to get back to work on the task at hand—finishing the sled Rassle, his spunky nephew, had begged and begged him to build so that he could win tomorrow morning's Glitterlit Downhill Sled Race. Sparky, wanting to please the son he never had, indulged nearly all of his nephew's whims and impulsive requests. With renewed determination, he crossed back to his workbench, picked up his familiar oak mallet, and hammered another wood peg into place.

Hitting his mark, the full weight of his mallet drove the peg straight into its hole. The heavy thudding sound of wood striking wood echoed off the rough-hewn rafters above. It was a familiar sound that made him feel useful and important. He glided his sandpaper-smoothed fingertips across the newly formed joint. Sleds are difficult to build, and no elf knew this better than Sparky. He gently placed his glasses, which had been squarely perched on the tip of his nose, closer to his eyes and bent over for a closer inspection.

"That's a snug, sure fit if there ever was one," he said to himself in a satisfied tone. He knew that if the sled's steering was crooked, disaster loomed for its rider. He stood the sled up on the heels of its runners and tested its steering. "A smooth tug to the right–check; now to the left–check. This will win the race faster than Rassle can count to three," he spoke with confidence. The Glitterlit Mountain foothills are steep, windy, and dangerous. They are greatly respected by all elves. Rassle had learned his sled-riding skills on those hills. He liked those hills the best.

Rassle, thusly named because he liked to wrestle, was now nearly 12 Christmases old, and he was growing faster than a pine sapling rooted in a knee-high barrel of fertilizer. Overly confident as usual, he'd already made bets with several of his elf friends that his new sled would take first place at the race. The pressure was on for Rassle to win tomorrow's race and for Sparky to finish building Rassle's unbeatable sled.

"KERR...ER...ERR...CHOO!" Without warning, Sparky sneezed and sprayed his workbench with a fine mist. Wiping his nose with his floppy glue rag, he sneezed again. His sneezing frustrated him beyond belief. Everytime he started painting he had to set down his brush to sneeze in messy bursts.

Last week was Sparky's most embarrassing episode yet–he sneezed directly into his paint can, splattering paint all over his apron and onto several other elves standing nearby. Needless to say, none of the other elves were a bit happy about it. In previous years he had painted millions of toys without even the smallest of sniffles. He was generally in excellent health and this sneezing just didn't make sense. With Christmas nearing, Santa couldn't afford to have him at less than his best, and Sparky knew it.

Knock, *knock*. *Knock*, *knock*. Near its handle, light taps came from outside the workshop door. Through it's knotholes Klee-Klee and Rassle peeked in at their favorite uncle.

Sparky quickly laid down his glasses, scooped up his mallet, and used it to answer their knocking with his own deliberate *knock*, *knock* against the corner of his workbench.

Over the years, these knocks had become a nightly ritual with Klee-Klee and Rassle that ended Sparky's day on its highest note. He waited for a moment, heard a few giggles, and then with his kindly voice invited the children to come in for their bedtime goodnights.

"All right you two. It's about that time, but before you sleep, I need your help."

Klee-Klee rounded the door first, sliding on her slippers like ice skates across the wood shavings. "Buh-dumb!" she blurted out as her bottom hit the floor. Klee-Klee's spirit was larger than life. Her laughter lit up the workshop and every corner of her uncle's heart. In Sparky's mind, she was his little snow princess beyond compare.

Sneaking in on all fours, Rassle carefully crept through the sawdust that had settled between the floor's cracks. He gave himself away as his bottom bobbed up and down in plain sight above the shop's boxes and workbench. Sparky, remembering how he often unsuccessfully snuck around his own mother's kitchen table to steal freshly baked molasses cookies, grinned ear to ear.

"Hello Klee-Klee. Where's that up-to-no-good older brother of yours tonight?" Rassle froze in place. For Rassle, there was no bigger thrill in life than catching his unflappable Uncle Sparky off guard.

"Are you there, Rassle?" Sparky called out to keep the game going. Trying to be as still as stone so he wouldn't give up his location, Rassle knew he couldn't hold his awkward position for long.

"Not sure where he is, Uncle Sparky. What do you need help with?"

Fighting back laughter, Sparky drew a long pause that only made Rassle's extreme discomfort worse. "It seems the sled I'm working on has a problem. Something to do with the steering I'm afraid. Klee, could you try it out?"

"Sure, I'd loooove to!" shrieked Klee-Klee.

"No you don't, KK!" commanded Rassle. "That's my job, Uncle Sparky!" Jumping to his feet and scampering across the floor, Rassle nearly tore up the workshop trying to reach his sled. Successfully foiling his surprise entrance, Sparky and Klee-Klee broke out laughing.

"Well good evening, nephew. So glad you could join us. What do you think?" he asked, pointing to the sled.

Rassle dropped the sled down on the floor, jumped on, and stretched himself out full-length on its finely sanded top. He yanked on the steering plank, pretending he was racing down Glitterlit Mountain.

"Yesssss. Perfect, Uncle Sparky!" he proclaimed as he sprang up to further admire his uncle's new masterpiece. "I'll win the race and become the most envied elf of the year. You're the best."

"Then it's finished, Rassle. You'll be unbeatable!" Sparky proudly proclaimed.

Feeling just a little left out at that moment, Klee-Klee begged, "Will you make me something special too?"

"Why of course Klee-Klee. I'd never, ever forget you! I've just completed the finishing touches on a sensational toy that will delight you to no end."

"Oh, what is it Uncle Sparky? Tell me, please tell me!" she pleaded.

Carefully choosing his words, Sparky smiled then answered, "Without entirely giving away my secret, this toy comes in a box and plays as it turns and turns."

Klee-Klee flashed Sparky a lost look, hoping to learn a few more details about the toy.

"Those are the only clues I'll give you, young lady." Sparky pursed his lips together to emphasize his point.

"But all gifts come in a box, Uncle Sparky. That's not a real clue!"

"Not like this box, Klee. You'll see soon enough," he promised.

"Super!" Klee-Klee exclaimed. Not able to contain her excitement, she broke out into a dance that sent her twirling. Her pigtails flew in all directions. Sparky stood entranced by her joyous movements–he could have watched her all night long. With his sticky glue rag, he dabbed his proud tearing eyes. Not only was Sparky Santa's most trusted elf, he was his most sentimental elf too.

"KERCHOOO!"

Out of nowhere, that tingling sensation from deep behind Sparky's nose exploded. His gigantic sneeze was only half caught by a corner of his soggy glue rag.

"Goodness, Uncle Sparky!" exclaimed Klee-Klee.

"Everything okay, Uncle?" asked a concerned Rassle.

"I think it's that darn paint. Something in it sends me off. I can't figure it out," he replied.

"Okay, okay you youngsters–time for bed. Tired elves are careless elves–the very worst kind. And you, Rassle, have a superspeedy sled to race in the morning. Time for a kiss, Klee." Sparky turned to Klee-Klee with open arms expecting his usual peck on the forehead.

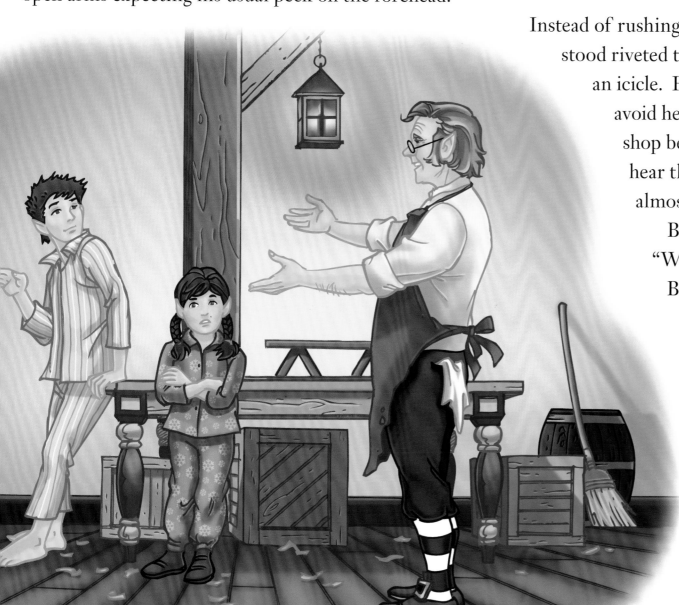

Instead of rushing into her uncle's arms, Klee-Klee stood riveted to the floor as if she'd turned into an icicle. Her eyes stared straight ahead to avoid her uncle's smiling face. The workshop became so quiet that Sparky could hear the reindeer snorting in their barn almost a quarter of a mile away.

Breaking the silence, Sparky asked, "What is it, Klee?"

Barely able to answer she muttered as though her jaw were frozen, "I'm too old for kisses now, Uncle Sparky."

"Oh really? And what about you, Rassle–are you too old for such nonsense as well, young sir?" quizzed the master elf.

"Well, actually I am, Uncle Sparky. My friends say they've outgrown the need for kisses and all that silly stuff, and, well, I'm in agreement–I have too." He pronounced this new policy as if decreed by Santa himself. "Everyone grows up, Uncle Sparky. We decided to grow up tonight."

"Is that right? KK and you, huh? Well, thanks for the update, Rassle. So Klee-Klee, you really think you're too old for a goodnight kiss?"

Rassle broke in, "Yes Uncle. She's 9. Its time for her to grow up too." Sparky tried to look Klee-Klee in the eyes, but she turned her head halfheartedly away. Sparky knew this night would eventually come–he just never guessed it would be tonight.

Pretending to grow stern, he cleared his throat in a gravelly manner and said, "Well even at 9 and 12, you're never too old for a good bedtime story. Take a seat and indulge a doting uncle."

Sparky picked up Klee-Klee and plopped her on the back end of the sled. Quick to follow, Rassle limberly sprang from a crate to land on the front of the sled. These two sensed they'd crossed the line and wondered if they'd angered him. Feeling tense, Klee-Klee bit her lower lip till it turned a pale shade of blue.

Not ever wanting to disappoint her uncle, she was nervous beyond belief.

She would never have opposed her uncle's wishes except that Rassle put her up to it.

    "Listen up. This will just take a moment, then off to bed with you two grown-ups." Klee-Klee was all ears. Acting older than he was, Rassle couldn't help but pick at the sled's slats and randomly glance around at the workshop–he was looking everywhere except into his uncle's knowing eyes.

    Sparky wisely began, "Now that you're grown up, I think it's time you both heard a seldom-told tale worth the telling." On his favorite stool he sat up straight and drew a long, measured breath.

"And so this tale goes..."

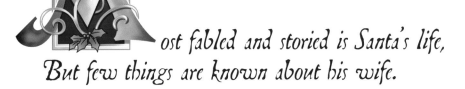ost fabled and storied is Santa's life,
But few things are known about his wife.

Long ago, folks called her Miss Suzie McEase,
The warmth of her smile could calm rough seas.

As a self-taught seamstress she mastered each thread,
She made clothes from scraps strewn about in her shed.

A poor girl reared with no food on the shelves,
She earned her good name, making clothes for cold elves.

She's pleasantly plump, and she dresses with care.
She perks up the toy shop with humor and flair.

Her laugh is infectious and sweeter than honey,
Her grandness of spirit, you can't buy with money.

She knows how to fix and run all the machines,
And cheer up sad elves, whatever the means.

She makes and collects cute dolls of all kinds,
And presses their clothes, so they're dressed to the nines.

Her strongest of skills is working with numbers.
She adds while awake and subtracts while she slumbers.

She'll hum a loud tune while she cooks a big meal,
But when down on her luck, she's tough as steel.

She gets her work done with a carefree manner.
Throughout the North Pole, she's the ultimate planner.

"Can I go to bed Uncle Sparky?" interrupted a squirming Rassle. "Your story is about boring girl stuff. I've got to get up very, very early to help with the wood chopping, and now my tummy is starting to ache." Usually riveted by his uncle's stories, Rassle was using every excuse he could think of to escape. Sparky blocked Rassle's attempt to bolt. Rassle got the message.

"Does Mrs. Claus really subtract while she sleeps Uncle?" Klee-Klee leaned closer to Sparky as if to hear an intimate secret about one's best friend. Sparky knew Mrs. Claus was Klee-Klee's all-time hero. If asked, she'd follow Mrs. Claus to the remotest iceberg.

"No, to going to bed Rassle; and yes, Klee-Klee, Mrs. Claus is excellent with numbers. At last count, she had more than three thousand dolls in her shop. She loves giving away dolls to playful little girl elves like you. She adds fun and subtracts boredom with every doll she gives."

To emphasize his point, Sparky lovingly tapped the tip of Klee-Klee's nose with his pinky finger. Klee-Klee let out a tiny giggle immediately quieted by a disapproving glare from Rassle.

"Well, I never heard of anyone who could subtract while asleep. Are you sure you got that part right Uncle Sparky?" Rassle had reached that age when every elf questions their elders.

"Sure as the spark in my name, Rassle."

Without further discussion, Sparky refitted his apron. Sparky's eyebrows then arched a bit as the tone of his voice grew more serious.

Yet no one is perfect, we all have our flaws.
This saying applies to the great Mrs. Claus.

She'll stretch out a tale, pull your leg for a spell,
And share Santa stories she ought not tell.

Like the very first time Santa worked Christmas Eve,
When he lacked a good suit and could not sew a sleeve.

It's hard to believe how Santa set out
With only one elf and so little clout.

For years as a boy, Santa lived without joys.
He barely could play, deprived of all toys.

From the simplest of things, he made his own fun,
And handcrafted toys that could pop, crank, or run.

Maturing to manhood, he got into gear.
He studied the weather, the globe, and reindeer.

And trained to achieve the perfect liftoff
In spite of high fever, strong winds, or bad cough.

With courage he vowed to deliver a gift
To every good child in a sleigh that was swift.

Yet his very first flight, in all of its glory,
Was almost a wreck, a near-tragic story.

Mrs. Claus ne'er told this story to me,
I lived it myself, I was just twenty-three.

With Santa's vast knowledge he still didn't know
Of the bleakest of storms, called the Black Arctic Snow.

When the snowstorm hit, Santa's nerves held steady,
His goals steadfast, but his suit wasn't ready.

He gravely misjudged the work it would take
To sew those fine stitches, for goodness' sake.

For when he bent over to load up his sleigh,
His suit ripped wide open, and in great dismay

To my cottage he tore, then he banged on my door.
From a snore I awoke to hear him implore,

"Please help me my friend, this sewing I hate,
Go find me a seamstress before it's too late!"

"Come on Uncle Sparky, now you're pulling our legs! Santa wouldn't rip through his suit." Rassle had a smart-alecky comment for everything. He shoved his teetering bottom off the sled and dropped to the floor, pretending that he ripped out the bottom of his pajamas. Klee-Klee jumped off the sled on the table to join in the joke. Sparky was not so amused.

With both hands, Rassle grabbed Klee-Klee's left ankle and started to pull her across the floor. Like a well-trained comedian, Klee-Klee reacted with an over-the-top yelp of pain. Klee-Klee and Rassle bumped foreheads and erupted into giggles. "Now look who's pulling whose leg, Uncle!" blurted Rassle. About to sneeze, Sparky was distracted. He lunged for his dappled glue rag lumped on the table and buried his face deep within its sticky folds.

KER-ER-ER-CHOOOO!

"KER-ER-ER-CHOOOO!" sneezed Sparky with tremendous force. Trying to determine if the paint made him sneeze, he picked up his loaded paintbrush and can and drew them closer for inspection.

"KERCHOOO!" Red drops of paint splattered across his shirt sleeves and apron.

"This paint will get the best of me yet!" muttered Sparky. "What would Santa say if he saw me this way?"

At that moment, Sparky felt a little embarrassed in front of his niece and nephew.

Rassle quipped, "He'd probably laugh a lot Uncle Sparky!" With both hands he tickled Klee-Klee.

"He probably would, Nephew." Sparky began to chuckle at his own expense and enjoy the elves' silliness. Losing his embarrassment, he swept up his paintbrush and stroked a random red brush mark across each of their cheeks.

"One messy elf deserves another!" proclaimed Sparky. Klee-Klee suddenly changed her mood and climbed back up onto the sled.

"What happened after Santa knocked on your cottage door, Uncle? Did he make Christmas that year?" questioned a worried Klee-Klee.

"Wise up KK. You can guess that he did. He wouldn't be Santa if he didn't." Rassle snorted out his words for double emphasis.

"And did you find a seamstress Uncle?" asked Klee-Klee.

Sparky, now clearly excited by this late-night banter, pressed on with his tale.

I braved the black blizzard nearly freezing to death,
Till I found Miss McEase, then I spoke out of breath,

"There's a man named Santa who needs your help now.
Bring thread and sharp needles and lots of know-how."

Not doubting my mission, she grabbed her red throw.
We trekked through the storm, sewing basket in tow.

But we soon lost our way on that bone-chilling night,
Till we glimpsed a faint glow from my cottage—a light!

Santa opened the door in his baggy attire.
As quick as he could, he then stoked the small fire.

As we warmed, Santa asked, "Will you mend this poor suit?
I really can't wait and I must find my boot,

Then fly above snowstorms and drifts that are deep
To deliver fine gifts to the children asleep."

"Dressed bright this dark night," said a thoughtful McEase,
"Your new suit needs fur so your body won't freeze."

She took her red throw and some fur from a rug,
And tested their strength with a pull and a tug.

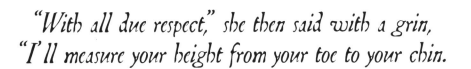

"With all due respect," she then said with a grin,
"I'll measure your height from your toe to your chin.

"Tonight a real suit will give you some power.
Stop pacing the floor, I'll need half an hour."

She measured her throw, then marked it and snipped.
As she finished his suit, Santa suddenly tripped.

Falling fast to the floor, he banged all about,
Not moving a muscle, he'd truly passed out.

Miss Suzie and I expected the worst.
Without doctor or nurse—Christmas was cursed!

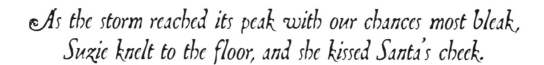

As the storm reached its peak with our chances most bleak,
Suzie knelt to the floor, and she kissed Santa's cheek.

Her tender kiss shook Santa Claus with such force,
That his eyes opened wide, then he stood up on course.

Not skipping a beat, he donned his red suit,
He loaded his sleigh, then pulled on his last boot.

To a shocked Miss McEase, he said "Thank you, you're great!
When I'm back in the morning, could we have our first date?"

Miss McEase didn't speak, but she nodded her head.
Santa knew in his heart that one day they'd be wed.

"In this red and white suit I'll be easy to see.
You're simply the best!" Santa said merrily.

He zipped round the globe on that foulest of nights,
Delivering his gifts on that first of all flights.

Now if you believe every kiss you should spurn,
Remember the kiss that saved Santa and learn...

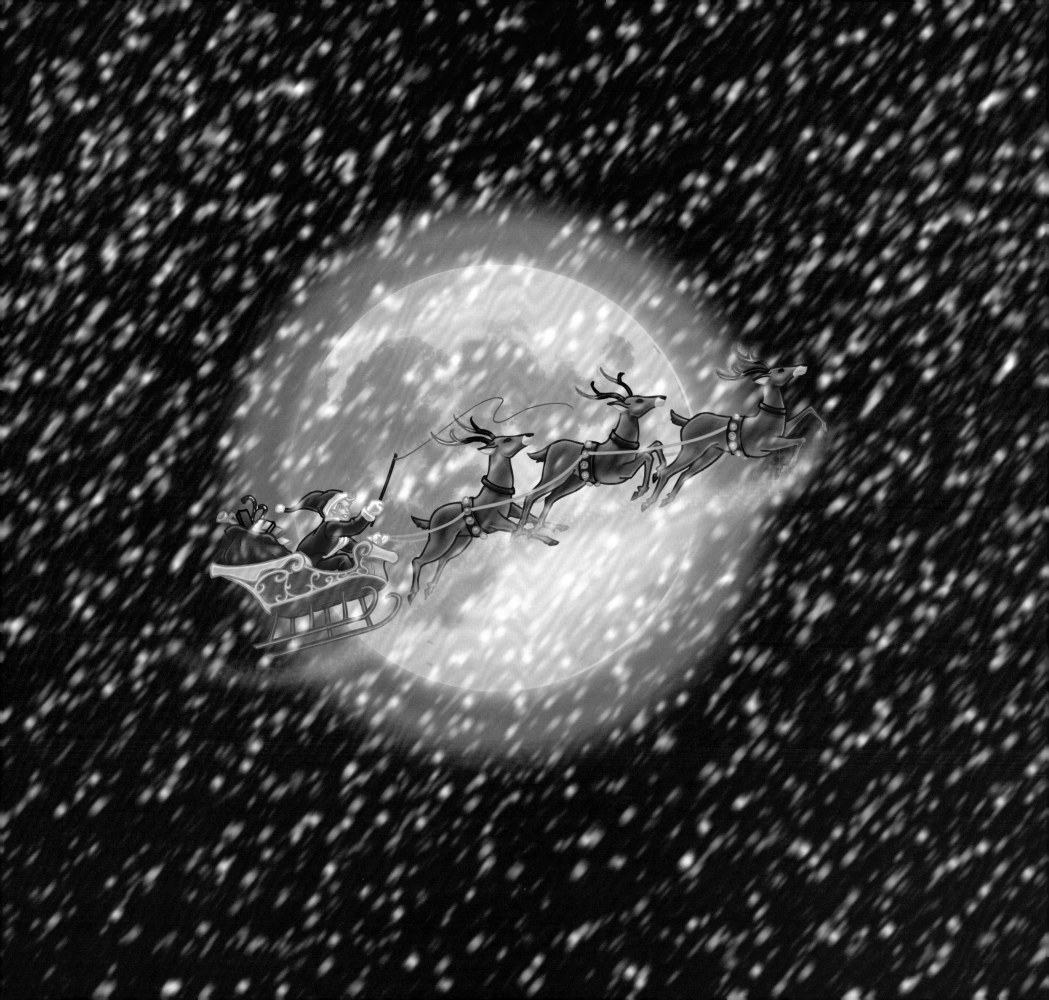

That he won't fall asleep, it's his strictest of laws,
Till his cheek gets a kiss from the great Mrs. Claus.

When Santa works wonders, it's thus because,
He's truly inspired by the great Mrs. Claus.

You're never too young or too old to show love.
It's what magic and soul and good things are made of.

This seldom-told story in your heart you must keep,
And kiss all your loved ones goodnight before sleep.

A calm hush came over the workshop. Even the ticktock sound from the clock seemed fainter. Sparky saw that Klee-Klee and Rassle had been touched by his story.

Klee-Klee was bundled up in her brother's arms and tucked into his lap. Rassle had finally relaxed. The story's meaning silenced him, until Klee-Klee accidentally elbowed his stomach.

"Ahhh, Sis!," groaned Rassle. He bounced Klee-Klee out of his lap and sat up straight as a plank, pretending to be unaffected by his uncle's story. "Ooo. . . that kissing is icky, gooey stuff, Uncle Sparky. Count me out for that!" he said with absolute certainty.

Not noticing her brother's abruptness, Klee-Klee said, "I didn't know Mrs. Claus did all that, Uncle. She was a brave and helpful person–she still is."
She longed to rush into her uncle's loving arms and plant a big sweet kiss on his forehead.

"Oh, I almost forgot about your gift Klee. Remember I told you that it plays as it turns? Well, here it is." Sparky brought it down from a high shelf. It was a shiny mahogany box about the height of a snowball. As Klee-Klee drew nearer Sparky lifted back the lid to expose two miniature figurines–they were a much younger Mr. and Mrs. Claus.

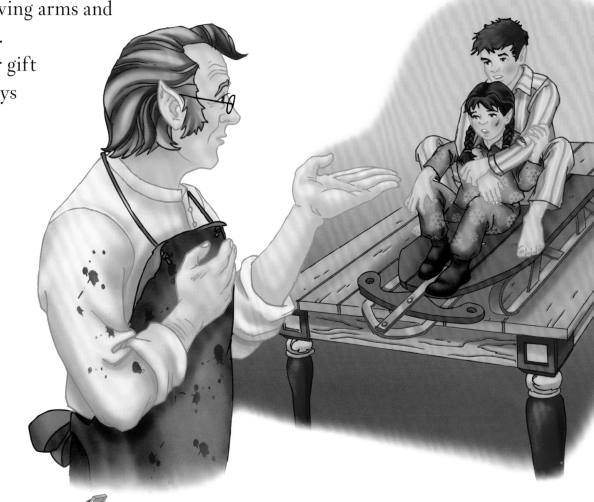

43

"Wind it up and see what happens." Klee-Klee did so with glee. The music played a sweet and lively tune just right for bedtime. She moved her fingers to the box's rhythm as if playing a piano. The figurines moved along different paths in opposite directions until at one point they came together for a kiss. Klee-Klee watched the figurines' hypnotic movements repeat until they came to a stop. She quickly rewound the box and set it on the table to play it again.

Not taking her eyes off the music box for a second, Klee-Klee cooed, "I could listen to this all night long, Uncle Sparky. And I love to watch them kiss. They're so cute. Thanks so much." Sparky felt taller than the tip of Glitterlit Mountain.

"Well Klee-Klee, another thing you may not know is that like Santa, I too can't sleep unless I get a peck of sugar on my brow." Sparky gestured for Klee to come closer. She hesitated, then gave in to her heart and bounced straight into her uncle's arms. Sparky gave her a big kiss and she kissed him right back.

"KƐ-KƐ-KƐƐƐƐR-CHOO!"

Without warning, Sparky released another gargantuan sneeze. He grabbed the glue rag from his workbench to wipe his nose again.

"When will this end?" Sparky demanded an answer from himself.

"Wait a second, Uncle. Let me smell that old rag." In a flash, Rassle swiped the rag out of his uncle's hand as if it were poisonous. He put it up to his nose and grimaced from its skunklike smell.

"I've got it Uncle! It's the glue. You're allergic to the glue! Some of the other elves I work with have the same problem. They were sneezing their elf caps off until we stopped using this new glue and switched to pine sap." Rassle glowed in his own cleverness. Sparky couldn't believe it.

He took back the glue rag from Rassle, held it up to his nose, and immediately let out another big sneeze.

"By Santa, you're right Rassle. You're a genius!"

With a sense of enormous relief, he gave Rassle a polar bear hug and a kiss on top of his head. Rassle returned the kiss in the same spot he'd kissed his uncle since he was two Christmases old.

"That didn't hurt a bit, did it Rassle?" chuckled Sparky. Sparky finally recognized the old Rassle he knew.

Klee-Klee tickled Rassle's side and then her uncle's. The three of them broke out into a chorus of laughter. They all understood how special it was to have one another.

Sparky hoped the goodnight kisses would continue to come, but, especially with Rassle, he knew those days were numbered.

Sparky casually gestured with a glance toward the door. The elves knew that was their bedtime cue. "Off to bed with you two merrymakers. Santa's Glitterlit Downhill Sled Race is first thing in the morning.

We all need our rest to be elf-excellent! Good luck Rassle. Sleep tight Klee-Klee."

Klee-Klee carefully picked up the music box, closed its lid, and tucked it under the top of her pj's to protect it. Her precious music box would play her to sleep. In unison, Klee-Klee and Rassle wished their uncle an exuberant "Goodnight!"

Before leaving the workshop, Rassle turned around one last time to admire his sled. Imagining the entire North Pole cheering him on with thunderous applause, he saw himself on the winner's stand getting his first place medal and a congratulatory handshake from Santa himself. Rassle looked at Sparky and with the proudest of smiles said, "With an uncle like you, who needs luck?" In his entire life, Sparky had never felt warmer inside than at that precise moment.

He watched the elves scamper off and disappear around the door. "With its runners waxed, it'll be ready for pickup early in the morning," he called out to remind Rassle. He tried out the sled's steering once more, then blew out the last candle that bathed the workshop in a warm yellow light.

As he climbed the creaky stairs to bed, he thought of Rassle winning the race and the new toys he'd start making from Santa's list—and from now on, doing it sneeze free! What a welcomed relief for Sparky and all those around him. Words from the tale he'd just shared with Rassle and Klee came back to him.

About the Author

Chris A. Shoemaker is a national award-winning columnist and first-time children's author.

The Great Mrs. Claus draws upon his decades-long tradition of playing Santa Claus with his family before audiences throughout the United States and abroad.

"Do I believe in Santa Claus? I most certainly do! My ruddy cheeks and aversion to hot weather are sure give-aways!" he chuckles. When not performing, a passion for collecting unusual art glass ornaments from faraway places keeps him in the Christmas spirit.

With more grandchildren on the way, Chris lives with his wife, Suzanne, in Southern California.

About the Illustrator

Since early childhood, Cesar De Castro has illustrated a multitude of fantastical characters and worlds.

He has drawn a wide range of projects that include comic books, animation, storyboards for screenplays, theme park attractions and several illustrated children's books. *The Great Mrs. Claus* strongly showcases Cesar's unique sense of North Pole play and elfin whimsy.

When not pushing his favorite pen, he enjoys time off playing the drums with his country western band and solving the trickiest of crossword puzzles.

Cesar lives in Southern California with his wife, children, and many spirited grandchildren.